I'm becoming

my mother

I'm becoming

my mother

An Anne Taintor Collection

Anne Taintor

CHRONICLE BOOKS

SAN FRANCISCO

Library of Congress
Cataloging-in-Publication
Data available.

ISBN 0-8118-4247-9

Manufactured in China.

Designed by Laura Crookston

Distributed in Canada by
Raincoast Books
9050 Shaughnessy Street
Vancouver, British Columbia V6P 6E5

10 9 8 7 6 5 4

Chronicle Books LLC
85 Second Street
San Francisco, California 94105

www.chroniclebooks.com

introduction

Domestically speaking, I was a late bloomer and an early retiree.

My mother saw no reason to teach her daughters the niceties of keeping the hearth. She had a better plan: we would marry men who could afford to hire us help. She always said, "It's just as easy to fall in love with a rich man as it is with a poor man." At eighteen I left home knowing how to wash and dry dishes, period.

To this day, I don't resemble anyone's domestic ideal, though I still deeply appreciate the pleasures of a well run home: floor swept and larder stocked. And I truly prefer a home-cooked meal to dinner in a fine restaurant any day. Lucky for me that I ended up with a man who cooks and cleans and shops. He can even find things in the refrigerator. So, domesticity is bliss . . . especially when someone else does it all for you.

Mom nearly had it right.

—Anne Taintor

let
the games
begin

mother was right...

this IS the happiest day of my life

all of her dreams had come true

what's my motivation here?

mortgage
payments
make
me
swoon

gosh,
he went well
with
her drapes

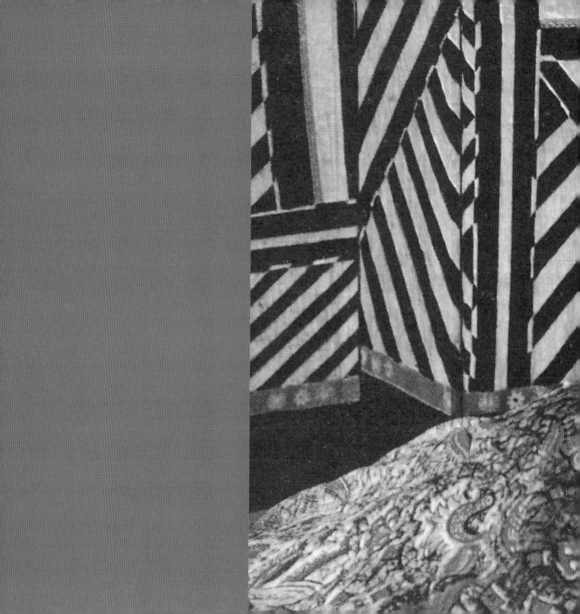

I *dream*
about
storage space

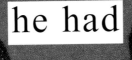

gee... he had an opinion

about everything

you're wearing *that?*

if only
she had bought it
when she saw it

cash
is for
amateurs

change

your

shoes...

change your life!

darling! let's get deeply into debt

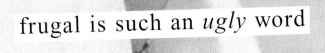
frugal is such an *ugly* word

she had made

yet *another*

wise shopping decision

she would show

them

consumer confidence

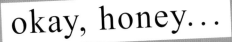

okay, honey...

tomorrow *you*

get to

wear

the dress

they put
the "funk"
in functional

am I
the last sane person
on this planet?

gee, thanks, Santa...

but I asked for take-out menus

another day

in

paradise…

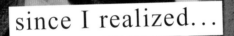

she had never guessed that cooking for one could be such a delight

it's a casserole, silly

does one serve *red* or *green* chili with a pinot noir?

don't worry, I'm a trained professional

her presentation was flawless

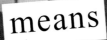
and son, that's what oedipal means

WOW!

I get to

give birth

AND

change diapers!

she always

enjoyed

receiving

gender-specific gifts

she liked to

stir things up

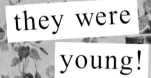

guess where I'm tattooed

he kind of enjoyed

taking orders

of *course* we're functional, honey... but more important– we're *funky*

she had done

a *fabulous* job

with him

she still missed

those

yuppie eastern greens

I am *devoted* to yardwork

I would *kill* for a riding mower

my garden

kicks

ass

I'm happy…

yet I'm aware

of the

ironic ramifications

of my happiness

if it's not

one thing,

it's your mother

I don't care *how* late your friends can stay out

because I'm the mother,

that's why

where did I go wrong?

am I

living

happily

ever

after

yet?

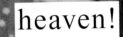

curtains!

slipcovers!

this must be

heaven!

I live in

fantasyland...

and I have oceanfront property!

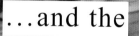

...and the
neighbors
are
darlings!

domestically

disabled

I refuse to let common sense cloud my judgment

I dreamed

my whole house

was clean…

Fran found
small talk
painless

as long as
she
limited herself
to appliances

gee, hon...

you'll make someone

a wonderful wife

some day

what I *really* want to do is direct